21st CENTURY CITIZEN

Genetic Engineering

Paul Dowswell

FRANKLIN
WATTS

Titles in this series:
AIDS
Animal Rights
Genetic Engineering
Immigrants and Refugees
Terrorism
World Hunger

© 2004 Arcturus Publishing Ltd

Produced for Franklin Watts by
Arcturus Publishing Ltd, 26/27 Bickels Yard,
151-153 Bermondsey Street, London SE1 3HA.

Series concept: Alex Woolf
Editor: Kelly Davis
Designer: Stonecastle Graphics
Consultant: Michael Reiss
Picture researcher: Shelley Noronha,
  Glass Onion Pictures
Illustrator: William Donohoe

Published in the UK by Franklin Watts.

British Library Cataloguing Publication Data
A CIP catalogue record for this book is
available from the British Library.

ISBN 0 7496 5463 5

Printed and bound in Italy

Franklin Watts – the Watts Publishing Group,
96 Leonard Street, London EC2A 4XD.

Picture acknowledgements
Camera Press 6; Popperfoto 11, 34 (Howard
Burditt); Rex Features 13 (Florence Durand/
Sipa Press), 16 (Ron Sachs), 21, 24 (Richard
Jones), 26 (Simon Roberts), 27 (Alexander
Caminada), 28 (Michael Ponomareff), 29 (James
Fraser), 37 (Ray Tang), 44 (Ben Dome); Science
Photo Library 4 (Makoto Wafuji/Eurelios),
5 (Alfred Pasieka), 12; Topham 1 and 38, 9
and cover, above (The Image Works), 14 (The
Image Works), 18, 23 (The Image Works), 25, 30
(The Image Works), 31 (Photri), 36 (Townsend
Dickinson), 40, 41 and cover, below, 43 (Polfoto),
45 (Rob Crandall).

Cover pictures
A US Federal Bureau of Investigation (FBI) agent loads
DNA samples in a DNA sequencer (above). Two of the
first goats to be cloned (below).

Note to parents and teachers
Some recommended websites are listed under
'Useful Addresses' at the back of this book.
Every effort has been made by the Publishers to
ensure that these websites are suitable for
children; that they are of the highest
educational value; and that they contain no
inappropriate or offensive material. However,
because of the nature of the Internet, it is
impossible to guarantee that the contents of
these sites will not be altered. We strongly
advise that Internet access is supervised by a
responsible adult.

Contents

1: What is Genetic Engineering?

Genetic engineering has been hailed as one of the greatest scientific discoveries of the twentieth century. It may change our lives as surely as the lives of past generations were changed by the invention of the wheel or machines powered by electricity.

But what exactly is it? In a nutshell, genetic engineering allows scientists to change the basic nature of nature itself. Do you want a dandelion that glows in the dark, like a fibre-optic light? It can be done. A gene that makes a jellyfish glow in the dark could be added to a dandelion. Do you want a human being with another 10 km per hour on top of his or her running speed? It could probably be done. Cheetahs and other fast-running animals have genes that help them get more oxygen into their blood, which in turn helps their muscles work harder. In the near future, parents wanting their child to be a world-class athlete could in theory

These fluorescent baby mice, the result of research at Osaka University, Japan, have a jellyfish gene which makes green fluorescent protein. This gene may be used to mark cancer cells in order to study cancer as it travels round the body.

PERSPECTIVES

'We are now standing in front of this plain of the whole human biology, the whole of human health, and we have in our hand as good a map as we could have.'

Genetic researcher Don Powell, Sanger Institute, Cambridge, UK, April 2003

have such a gene added to their baby when he or she was still an embryo in the womb.

This book shows how genetic engineering works, and explains what uses are currently being made of it, and what could be done with it in the future. The book also asks what we should, and should not, do with this extraordinary new technology.

What are genes?

To understand what genetic engineering is, you need to understand what genes are. From tiny bacteria to towering oak trees, every living thing on Earth is made of cells. Bacteria have only one cell, while oak trees have many trillions. Your body has around 100 trillion cells. Despite being very tiny, cells are very complicated. Each one has a control centre called a nucleus, which tells that cell what to do. (So, sweat cells produce sweat, brain cells link together to think, muscle cells pull.) Within each nucleus are rod-shaped structures called chromosomes. The number of chromosomes differs between all living things. For example, human cells have 46 chromosomes, while cats have 38. Chromosomes are made up of tightly wound coils of chemicals called DNA (deoxyribonucleic acid). The DNA contains genes, and it is genes that make every living thing look and behave as it does. The genes, taken together, are known as the genome.

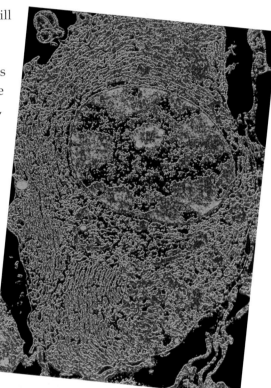

A cross-section through a normal human cell, showing the nucleus in orange and blue.

The genes of an oak tree tell it to grow tall and put down deep roots, and what sort of shape its leaves should be. The genes of a tiger tell it to grow its magnificent stripy fur coat, and hunt other animals. Your genes, among thousands of other things, dictate the colour of your eyes, whether you have straight or curly hair, and whether you will be tall or short. (This is not the whole story though. Your physical and mental characteristics also depend on your diet, your health as a child, and other environmental

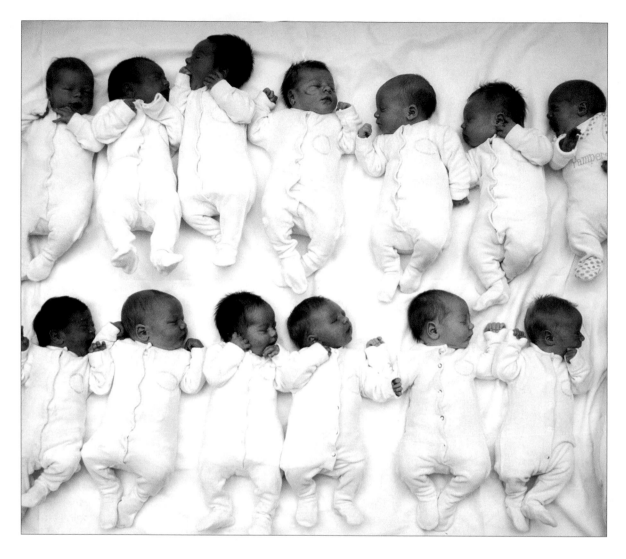

influences.) Not all genes are beneficial. You may have a gene for bad eyesight, or one that will lead you to develop a disease in your twenties or thirties.

Newborn babies' future lives are greatly influenced by their genes, but their upbringing and environment also play a vital part.

The 'book of life'

DNA contains a sequence of four different chemicals, A, T, C and G (Adenine, Thymine, Cytosine and Guanine) called bases. These bases add up to a particular gene, which in turn makes up a recipe, or code, for each living thing. As you would expect, this recipe is extremely complicated. Most genes have around 3,000 bases in their recipes. The longest has around 2.5 million. The human genome has just over 3 billion bases. To put it very simply, imagine the genome as a book. The chromosomes are chapters within that book, the genes are the words, and the bases make up the letters.

What are genes made of?

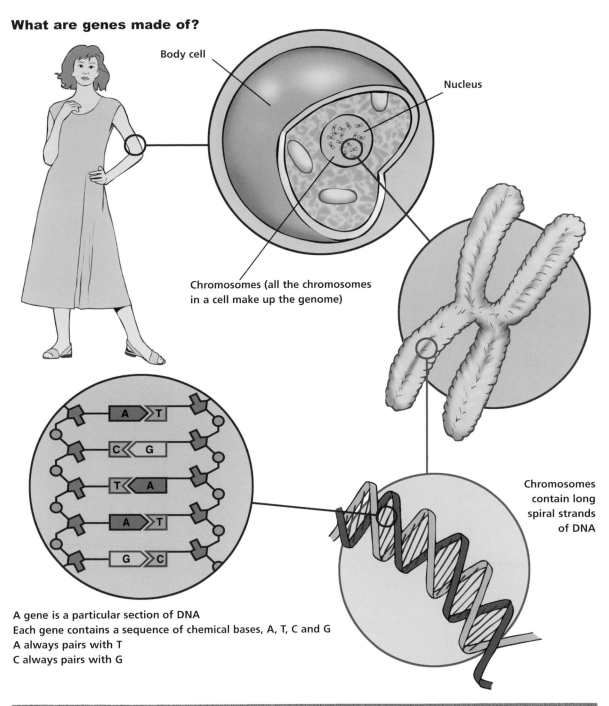

Body cell

Nucleus

Chromosomes (all the chromosomes in a cell make up the genome)

Chromosomes contain long spiral strands of DNA

A gene is a particular section of DNA
Each gene contains a sequence of chemical bases, A, T, C and G
A always pairs with T
C always pairs with G

PERSPECTIVES

'We used to think our fate was in the stars. Now we know, in large measure, our fate is in our genes.'

James Watson, genetic pioneer and Nobel Prize winner, Time magazine, USA, March 1989

Why alter genes?

Genetic engineering gives us the ability to alter genes in living things, in order to make them look or behave differently. The reasons for wanting to do this are almost endless. Here are a few possible uses for genetic engineering:

• People with an inherited disease, such as cystic fibrosis, have this condition because they have one or more genes that cause it. They inherited this gene from one or both of their parents and there is a high chance they will pass it on to their own children. If the genes of their children could be altered before they were born, they would not inherit the condition.

• Farm animals, such as chickens, can have the genes removed that cause them to have feathers. Featherless chickens would save farmers' money, as they would not need to ventilate battery farms to keep their chickens from getting too hot. Also, featherless chickens would not have to be plucked before they were eaten.

• Bacteria can be genetically engineered to produce medicines. Insulin, which is used to treat people with diabetes, is already produced this way.

• Some crops, such as cotton, are frequently destroyed by insects. Cotton can be genetically engineered to produce a poison that kills these insects before they can do much damage.

The possibilities offered by genetic engineering are extraordinary, but just because something *can* be done it does not mean it *should* be done. For example, many people feel it is wrong to deprive a chicken of its feathers for the sake of cheaper and more easily prepared food. It may be possible to remove an inherited disease by genetic engineering, but it may also be

PERSPECTIVES

'Geneticists now have the raw data for the complex blueprint of [a human] life; the next step is to work out how the pieces fit together... and why that human is victim of a range of different afflictions.'

Tim Radford, science journalist, Guardian *newspaper, UK, April 2003*

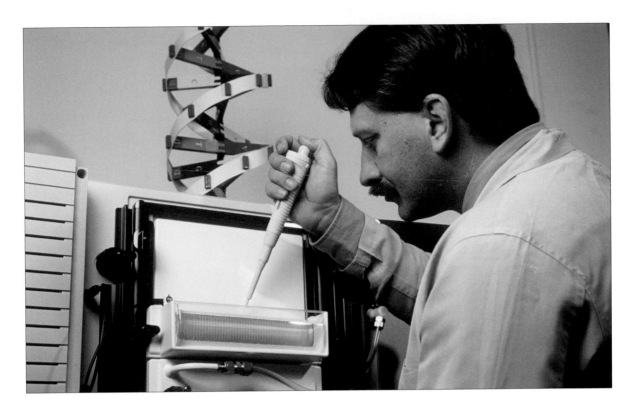

possible to make babies more intelligent or more beautiful. Would it be right to make these changes too? These issues are explored in greater detail later on.

A US Federal Bureau of Investigation (FBI) agent loads DNA samples in a DNA sequencer. Increased genetic knowledge has had a major impact on criminal investigation techniques.

The wider world of genetics

This book's main focus is on how scientists can alter genes to make living things different. But advances in genetics have also had an impact on other areas of science. For example, the issue of cloning hit the headlines in 1997 when scientists at the Roslin Institute in Scotland announced they had cloned a sheep, named Dolly. The news caused a sensation all around the world – for most people cloning was a subject only found in science fiction. The point of cloning animals is a practical one. A good strong sheep or pig could be reproduced many times, and provide a farmer with a healthy product. But there was an immediate concern that some people would try to clone themselves or other humans. One American insurance company even offers celebrities a compensation package to cover expensive legal action in case a fan tries to clone them. This is brought about by a fear that obsessive fans would try to 'own' their own versions of the stars they adore. Cloning, in animals, is still a science in its infancy, and only time will tell whether it develops into anything truly useful to the world.

Another recent area of genetic research is DNA testing, where small samples of body fluid or tissue found at the scene of a crime can be used to identify a culprit, or clear the name of someone wrongly accused of committing that crime. A New York-based organization called The Innocent Project uses genetic evidence to fight miscarriages of justice. To date, they have saved several condemned men from death row.

DNA testing can also be used to detect whether someone is likely to get a particular illness, and to confirm whether two people belong to the same family. Such testing could soon be made remarkably easy by the development of 'gene chips'. These small diagnostic tools can indicate a risk of illness, and also point to the most suitable drugs needed to treat that illness. Such knowledge throws up some thorny problems. For example, if a genetic test shows that a teenager is likely to develop a fatal illness in middle age, would it be right to deny that person life insurance?

How do we know about genes?

The idea that particular characteristics can be passed on from one generation to another has been familiar since the days of the Ancient Egyptians, when farmers would select only the strongest animals to breed or seeds from the biggest plants to sow. Unknowingly, they were passing on the best genes as they improved their crops and livestock. The fact that children usually look like one or both of their parents also told people that something of themselves was being passed on to their offspring. Around 2,000 years ago, people in the area that is now India realized that parents could pass on particular diseases to their children.

But it was only in the nineteenth century that scientists began to find out how this happened. The English naturalist Charles Darwin and the Austrian monk Gregor Mendel developed the sciences of evolution and inheritance. Mendel began the first work in explaining the process of inheritance – the mechanisms by which living things pass on their characteristic features to their offspring. In evolution, Darwin showed how successive generations of animals and plants can gradually change, over millions of years, to adapt to their environment.

In the early twentieth century, improvements in microscope design led biologists to discover chromosomes and genes within the nucleus of a cell. They recognized that chromosomes and genes were the structures that passed on characteristics from a parent to its offspring. And by the 1940s, it was accepted that chromosomes and genes existed in a substance called DNA. The major breakthrough came in 1953 when James Watson and Francis Crick, acting on previous research by Rosalind Franklin, realized that DNA was a long double spiral, or helix, of four chemicals. Once they had discovered this, they understood how the DNA chemical code worked. Most significantly, the shape of the double spiral explained:

• How DNA manages to copy itself when a cell divides. (Cells in your body are dividing all the time – when you grow as a child, when your body heals after an injury, and when new cells replace old ones in a constant process of keeping your body healthy.)

• How DNA from a male and female plant or animal is passed on to their offspring. In humans, for example, reproductive cells (sperm and egg) have 23 chromosomes rather than the usual 46. When a sperm and egg join to make a baby, the 23 female and 23 male chromosomes make a cell with 46 chromosomes. This then divides until it forms a baby, which inherits characteristics from both its parents.

Watson and Crick's discovery was one of the most significant of the century. For, once scientists understood what DNA looked like, they could set about learning how to understand it and manipulate it. This is the basis of genetic engineering.

The Austrian botanist Gregor Mendel (1822-84) was an Augustinian monk and a teacher of natural history. His famous law of heredity, resulting from his study of the common garden pea, was first published in 1866 but received no attention until 1900.

James Watson (left) and Francis Crick (right) with their model of the DNA double spiral.

CASE STUDY

Gene science is big business. There is keen rivalry between those who want to research genetics to make money, and those whose motives are advancing scientific knowledge and improving people's lives. In Britain the Sanger Centre in Cambridge set out to map the human genome, declaring that it would make this information freely available to all. But in the USA, a company called Celera Genomics developed a faster method of mapping the genome, and announced that it would try to patent particular gene sequences it discovered. This meant that other scientists would have to pay them if they made use of this information. The Sanger Centre and Celera Genomics both completed their work at the same time. Because of their rivalry, mapping the human genome was an endeavour marred by ill-feeling. Nevertheless, when the project was nearing completion the two rivals agreed to a limited degree of co-operation. (The Sanger Centre and Celera Genomics were not the only companies to do this work – countries all around the world participated.)

Up to the present

Many discoveries followed in the wake of Watson and Crick's work, especially in the field of diagnostic medicine. ('Diagnostic' means discovering what is wrong with someone who is ill or who has a disability.) Scientists were able to confirm that particular genes caused specific conditions, such as sickle cell anaemia (a severe blood disorder) or cystic fibrosis. They were also able to identify which genes did this.

In 1990, the Human Genome Project began to map (record) every gene in every chromosome in a human cell. In April 2003 the project was completed. If printed out, the 3 billion letter code would take up about 750,000 sheets of letter-size computer printer paper, but it is also conveniently available via the Internet.

This information can now be used in all kinds of extraordinary ways. The main areas of development, debate and concern are in medicine, genetic enhancement (that is, the 'improvement' of children by giving them extra genes), and genetically modified food. These topics are covered in more detail in the next three chapters of this book.

A sample of the code from the Human Genome Project, showing sequences of the four base chemicals A, T, C and G.

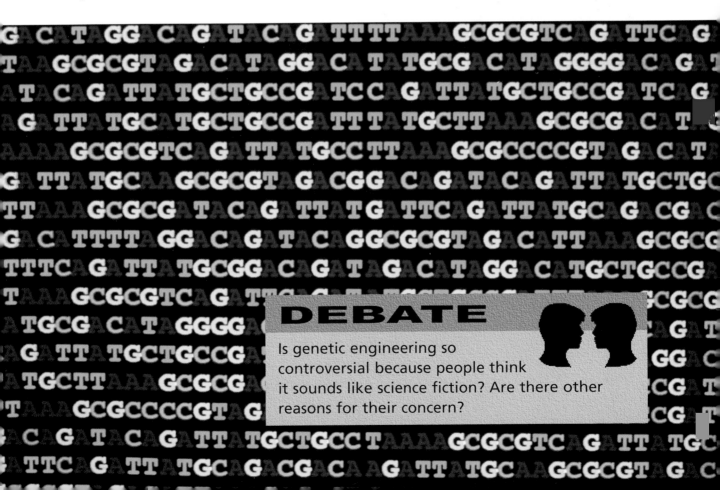

DEBATE

Is genetic engineering so controversial because people think it sounds like science fiction? Are there other reasons for their concern?

2: Medicine and Health

Predicting whether or not you would develop a crippling or fatal disease used to be a job for a sorcerer or fortune-teller. But it may soon be possible for a doctor to predict your health in the years to come. This is because illness lurks within people's genes. Examining a person's genetic code can reveal his or her medical future. This future, however, is not set in stone. The onset of a disease may be triggered by lifestyle choices, such as smoking, drinking or poor diet.

Such knowledge can be frightening, especially as some genes carry an almost certain sentence of early death. But it is not all doom and gloom. Genes connected with health often only indicate a predisposition (tendency) towards a certain illness, rather than an absolute certainty of its onset. We still do not fully understand how much people's environment and personal

Dr J. Craig Venter (right), president of the Celera corporation, at a press event held to explain the sequencing of the human genome. He is accompanied by Mark Adams (left), chief genetic researcher at Celera. Knowledge of the completed genome will revolutionize medicine over the coming decades, giving us new tests and drugs for previously untreatable diseases.

J. CRAIG VENTER   FRAN

circumstances influence their health. For example, it is highly likely that smoking causes lung cancer in people who have a genetic predisposition to this illness. If such a person did not smoke, he or she would probably not develop this cancer. Likewise, people without this genetic disposition may be able to smoke heavily throughout their lives, and not develop cancer either (though they may die of other smoking-related illnesses).

The science of predicting and identifying illness is called diagnostics and this is only one area of medicine that will be affected by our greater understanding of genetics. Scientists have realized that if a certain set of genes makes a person likely to get a particular illness, then it may be possible to repair or replace those genes to prevent that illness occurring. This knowledge will probably have a major impact on medicine over the next 50 years in richer countries. Nonetheless, the future of genetic engineering and medicine is still uncertain. The more we discover, the more we realize there is to know.

Stem cells

When an egg cell is first fertilized in one of the mother's fallopian tubes, it divides into two, then four, then eight cells. After that, it multiplies again and again until it eventually reaches an enormous total – a hundred million, million cells. When the embryo is about four weeks old, the cells begin to form themselves into specific parts of the body, such as arms, eyes or digestive system. The cells do this because their genetic code instructs them to become particular types of cell. (Each human cell, from skin cells to brain cells, nerves and hair, does its own vital job.)

However in the earliest stages of life, before the cells take on particular roles, they are called 'stem cells', and they can become any part of the body – from brain cells to muscle. Once they have become particular cells, they switch off the ability to become any other type of cell. If the stem cell mechanism could be engineered to switch itself back on, then the body could grow new arteries or new nerve endings – or even a new eyeball to replace one lost in an accident. This is the basic science behind one revolutionary new area of genetic engineering.

The possibilities here are extraordinary. Slowly worsening diseases, such as Parkinson's, Alzheimer's or multiple sclerosis, could be delayed or even reversed. Brain injuries caused by

CASE STUDY

'One cell bank derived from a single embryo produces enough neurons to treat 10 million Parkinson's disease patients.'

Thomas Okarma, president of US biotech giant Geron, talking to the BIO 2003 conference on the benefits of stem cell research, June 2003

The actor Michael J. Fox, who suffers from Parkinson's disease, at a US Senate subcommittee hearing on the benefits of stem cell research.

strokes could perhaps be repaired. Patients paralysed by a broken back might eventually be cured. (Experiments on paralysed rats with broken spinal columns have shown very encouraging results.) Other illnesses, especially those associated with old age, such as failing hearing and eyesight, and arthritis, could be tackled. One great advantage of a breakthrough in stem cell research is that encouraging people's cells to repair their own bodies would be much cheaper than other current therapeutic treatments, which often involve complex and highly expensive procedures.

However, this area of genetic research is very controversial, because the best and most effective way scientists can understand more about it is by working on the stem cells of embryos. These are usually those left over from fertility treatment patients. In some fertility treatments, several of the hopeful mother's eggs are fertilized outside the body, and only one or two embryos are put back in the womb. Research on the spare embryos results in their inevitable destruction. Some people think this is wrong. They argue that carrying out this research means, in effect, killing unborn children. Because of these objections, considerable restrictions have been placed on this revolutionary new area of medicine.

Nevertheless there may be ways around this problem. At the time of writing, research is being carried out into free-floating stem cells found in the mother's amniotic fluid (the watery substance that surrounds a baby in the womb). This would neatly side-step the ethical problem of using embryo stem cells.

It is becoming widely understood that stem cells will have great medical value in the future. In some countries, new parents are already asking for blood samples from their baby's umbilical cord to be frozen and held in storage. Like amniotic fluid, this blood also contains stem cells that could be used for any future treatment of that child.

Drug production

A less controversial area of genetic engineering in medicine is drug production. Until 20 or so years ago, all drugs were made

CASE STUDY

'...we... can't afford to be casual about what we do with nascent [very early] human life. And we don't want to become a society in which nascent human life, what you and I once were in our earliest stages, is regarded as a mere natural resource.'

Leon Kass, US presidential adviser on ethical issues, discussing stem cell research using human embryos, on the PBS programme 'Now with Bill Moyers', July 2003

from plants and chemicals, and in some cases animal products. Now, genetic engineering has given drug manufacturers two other methods of producing their goods – recombinant DNA technique and pharming. The recombinant DNA technique involves inserting useful DNA into the DNA of fast-breeding bacteria. These bacteria then produce proteins that can be used as medicines. This technique has been used since 1981 to manufacture insulin, an essential drug for diabetics.

Pharming uses genetically altered animals or plants to make drugs. Sheep, for example, have been used to make a drug called alpha-1-antitripsin, which they produce in their milk. It is hoped that this drug will be used in the treatment of cystic fibrosis, a disease that causes the lungs to become clogged with mucus. Plants such as maize and tobacco can also be used to produce substances that can be processed to use in medicines. Many vaccines are now produced using genetically engineered ingredients.

Genetic engineering in action. These culture dishes contain gene corrected T-lymphocytes – white blood cells that play a vital role in the body's immune system.

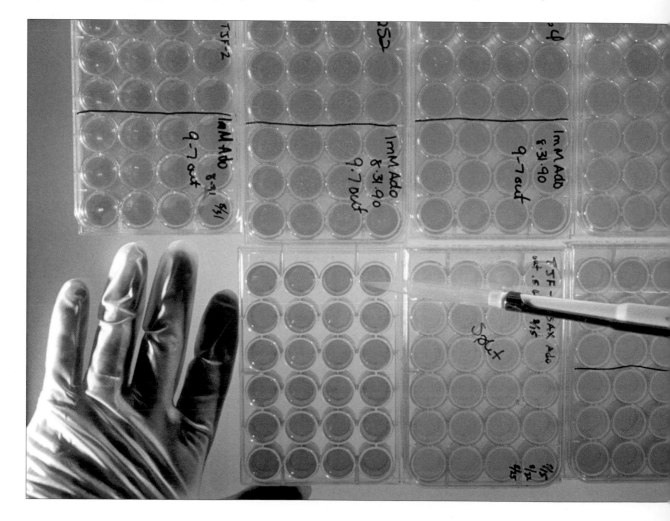

This research has prompted fears of people being used as 'drug factories', especially since a research department at Baylor University, Texas, USA, tried to patent the concept of a 'pharmwoman' – a genetically engineered human who would produce medically beneficial substances in her breast milk. In some poor countries people already offer their body organs for sale, so they might also consider allowing themselves to be used as human drug producers.

Gene therapy

Another extraordinary technique, still in its early stages of research and development, is that of gene therapy. In somatic gene therapy, healthy genes are introduced into a patient's body to try to replace unhealthy genes. This method has been tried as a cure for cystic fibrosis. The unhealthy lung cells, which produce too much mucus, are attacked by a genetically modified virus that replaces their chromosomes with healthy genes. These

Somatic gene therapy – a cure for cystic fibrosis?

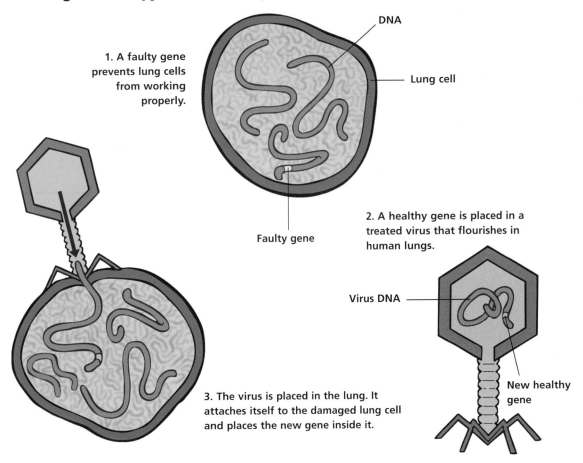

1. A faulty gene prevents lung cells from working properly.

DNA

Lung cell

Faulty gene

2. A healthy gene is placed in a treated virus that flourishes in human lungs.

Virus DNA

New healthy gene

3. The virus is placed in the lung. It attaches itself to the damaged lung cell and places the new gene inside it.

CASE STUDY

Since the late 1990s, the Necker Hospital in Paris has been one of the leading medical pioneers in genetic research. Revolutionary somatic gene therapy trials on children with Severe Combined Immunodeficiency Disease (SCID) went remarkably well. Nine children were cured of this life-threatening condition. But another child, a boy, went on to develop leukaemia (cancer of the blood). This was almost certainly as a result of the therapy. The most likely cause was the virus used in the therapy (see diagram on page 19). This had an unexpected side-effect, activating another gene in the boy's body which set off his leukaemia.

healthy genes should enable the lung cells to produce normal amounts of mucus. For the moment, there is one major drawback with this technique. The lung cells only live a short time, so the treatment has to be repeated regularly for it to be beneficial.

Another technique, germline gene therapy, involves treating the genes in the body's so-called germ cells – the sperm and egg needed to start a new human life. (The word 'germ' is actually derived from a Latin word meaning 'a seed'.) Here the defective gene is replaced by its correctly functioning version before conception (the beginning of a life) occurs. In effect this means preventing a disease before it has even begun to develop. This technique could prevent crippling inherited diseases being passed from parents to their children.

The germline method is controversial because it permanently alters the genetic code of the person who is treated. Any children resulting from this treatment would also have this altered genetic code. So far, germline therapy has only been tried on animals. In many countries it is illegal to try this on humans. For the moment, there is still too great a possibility of producing a deformed baby.

So far, neither somatic nor germline gene therapy have lived up to expectations. But these are early days in the genetic revolution. In ten years' time, the prospects may be much brighter.

Other areas

Genetic engineering offers other exciting prospects in the field of medicine. One area is skin cells which can be grown to treat burns or to help cancer patients who have been disfigured by their condition. (Genetically engineered skin is usually better, cheaper and promotes quicker healing than conventional artificially grown skin.)

Another area being developed is that of engineering animals to provide new body parts for humans who need organ transplants. One of the greatest problems facing a transplant patient is that the new organ, taken from the body of a donor, is often rejected by the patient's own body. This is because the immune system is programmed to attack anything that is not part of that person's body. Rejection provides a good defence against germs but causes many problems when it comes to transplanted organs. However, if a pig could be engineered to grow a human liver from the cells of the person needing a transplant, then the liver would not be attacked by the patient's immune system because it would be recognized as part of the person's own body. So far, though, using animal body parts in surgery has had unexpected consequences. For example, a few patients have developed Creutzfeldt-Jakob disease (an illness that can be passed on to people who have eaten BSE-infected beef) through surgical procedures such as corneal transplants.

These cloned piglets have been created for research into animal to human transplants.

Forever young?

Along with the treatment of disease, another area of human health that could be affected by genetic engineering is the process of ageing. Altering people's DNA could enable them to live much longer. This may sound like science fiction, but – thanks to scientific research – it now has a basis in reality. Throughout our lives, our body cells continue to renew themselves. Ageing happens when this renewal process stops working properly. This is why people's bodies begin to show signs of ageing, and their strength and senses start to fade. Cells can be genetically engineered to help slow down this deterioration. Another potential procedure would involve healthy cells being taken from various parts of a person's body, such as heart and brain, when he or she was a child. The cells could then be used to repair these organs in later life.

Keeping people looking young is big business. Cosmetic surgery and other anti-ageing measures, from skin creams to botox treatment, make millions of dollars. If genetically engineered anti-ageing therapies prove to be safe and effective, they will undoubtedly be in great demand. But the possibilities offered by such medical advances raise major ethical problems. If these treatments are so expensive that only a few very wealthy people can afford them, then such therapies will remain a scientific curiosity and society will become even more divided. On the other hand, if anti-ageing therapies become cheap enough to be available to a large number of people, serious social problems could be created by older people keeping jobs, houses and resources needed by the rest of their country's population.

CASE STUDY

Cancer is caused when a body cell begins to grow out of control, multiplying wildly and causing a tumour to develop. Recent genetic research at the US National Cancer Institute and New York's Columbia University has shown that a gene called p-53 keeps cells under control. Cancers happen when p-53 does not work properly. If this gene can be replaced by a healthy p-53 then it may be possible to prevent the cell malfunctioning. The problem here, though, is that cancer is usually caused by a combination of factors, rather than by a single defective cell. Nevertheless, perhaps this knowledge will contribute to a long-awaited cure for cancer?

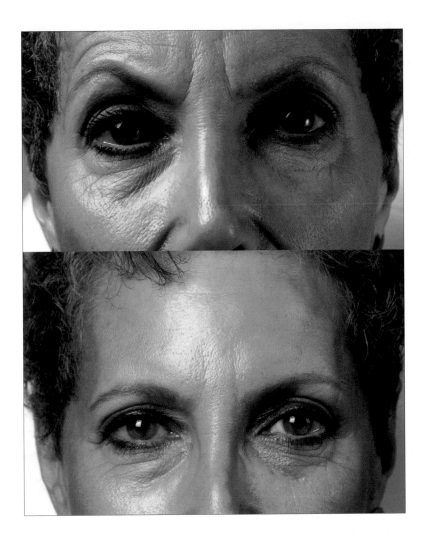

Anti-ageing cosmetics and treatments, such as this illustration of the effects of botox injections to remove facial lines, have been a huge commercial success. This has encouraged financial investment in research into delaying ageing through genetic engineering.

DEBATE

Research into genetic medicine techniques is very expensive. Other areas of medical research, such as cheap, low-technology cures for common killers like cholera, would save far more lives in the short term. Should scientists devote their time and resources to research that is likely to produce medicine for all today? Or should they focus on cutting-edge medical techniques which are likely to benefit only the wealthy few in the near future but could perhaps help the wider population in the longer term?

3: Making 'Better' People

Some people are already starting to imagine a future in which parents will be able to order up babies to their exact genetic requirements – including, for example, height, looks, build, intelligence, musical ability. Although such ideas are currently in the realm of science fiction, they may become reality in the not-too-distant future. And many genetics experts are deeply troubled by the idea of using genetic science to change a person's gender, appearance, intelligence or character.

'Designer babies'

We know that individual genes are responsible for a person's appearance, and even their intelligence and ability. The process of changing these genes, known to scientists as 'human genetic enhancement', and more commonly as 'making designer babies', is similar to that being developed in germline therapy (see page 20). Genes are changed in the egg or sperm used to make a baby.

It may even be possible to grow such designer babies in their own artificial wombs. At Cornell University, Ithaca, New York State, researchers are working on an artificial womb lining which would allow the busy mother of a genetically enhanced baby the option of not having to carry her child for nine months.

Genes certainly seem to affect human character. Intelligence, personality, humour, ambition, even our tendency towards personal happiness – a 'sunny nature' – are probably built into our genes, just like our height and hair and eye colour. A special

Parents may have many reasons for wanting to choose their child's gender. For instance, in some cultures male children are valued more highly than female children. In China, where the government has tried to control population growth by enforcing a one-child policy, many female babies are put up for adoption. Here, eight little girls in Guangzhou province wait for new parents. Genetic science enables medical workers to determine the sex of the child at conception.

report in the magazine *American Psychologist* concluded that in half the cases it studied, there was a clear link between the intelligence of the child and his or her parents. Many scientists think this suggests intelligence is passed on through the parents' genes to the child.

Dark future?

The science exists, or almost exists, for this to happen – so much so that academics and other commentators on human genetic engineering are already worrying about the likely consequences. Lee Silver, Professor of Molecular Biology at Princeton University, USA, envisages a super-race of genetically enhanced children of the rich. (Such genetic treatment would be expensive, and therefore only available to a privileged few.) With healthier bodies and sharper brains, such children would have an inbuilt advantage over their non-genetically enhanced peers. Those who could not afford such enhancement would be of lesser intelligence, and subject to the usual run of human diseases. Such an elite class, says Silver, would take all the best jobs and only marry among themselves. Eventually, he predicts, they would become an entirely separate species.

Babies can be 'designed' to help cure their siblings' health problems. Zain Hashmi (centre) suffers from a potentially fatal genetic blood disorder. His illness could be cured with stem cells (see pages 15-17) harvested from the umbilical cord of a sibling. However the new sibling's embryo would have to be selected by means of genetic engineering. Here, Zain and his parents celebrate a court ruling in their favour, allowing them to proceed with this controversial treatment.

But not everyone agrees with this bleak view of the future. Among them is American academic Steven Pinker, who is Johnstone Professor of Psychology at Harvard University. He thinks such claims are exaggerated. Genes for particular talents, whether playing the piano, doing mathematical calculations or pole-vaulting, have yet to be specifically isolated. Besides, from what we understand of the way genes work, it is almost impossible to find one gene which works on its own. Talents and abilities are invariably the result of many genes working together in a way we do not yet fully understand.

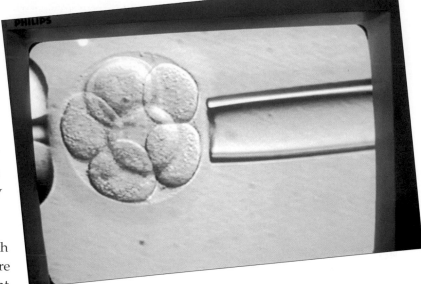

Embryo cells being manipulated on a TV monitor screen.

Besides, some experiments with animals have revealed a more sinister side to gene enhancement. Recently, mice 'enhanced' with a gene for greater learning and memory did indeed show some improvement in laboratory tests. But the gene also interacted with their other genes to make the mice more sensitive to pain. Even the most ambitious parents would surely hesitate to inflict such a fate upon their own child.

It could well be that the whole issue of human character and intelligence is far too complicated to solve by means of genetic engineering. Besides, as Pinker also points out, most people have an inbuilt suspicion of the 'unnaturalness' of genetically enhanced children, and the procedure they would have to go

PERSPECTIVES

'The rich would benefit from genetic engineering far more than the poor. And the gap in power, wealth and education that currently divides both our society and the world at large would be written into our very biology.'

Bill McKibben, US journalist, in his book Enough: Genetic Engineering and the End of Human Nature, *2003*

CASE STUDY

Gene manipulation is far from simple, and may produce quite unexpected results. For example, in the 1990s a pig with a human growth gene was reared by the US Department of Agriculture, in one of its research centres. The intention was to produce a much bigger pig, and therefore more pork. But the experiment was a failure. The animal, known as 'Pig 6707', was very hairy, lethargic, and suffered from arthritis. It did grow very large, but it could barely stand up.

How much of this girl's talent at playing the flute is due to nature and how much is due to nurture?

through to bring such children into the world. Most would prefer to have children by the usual method.

Nature and nurture

Genetic research has confirmed the importance of genes in people's characters and their physical appearance and capabilities. But it is also clear that an individual's upbringing, lifestyle and surroundings can be just as important as his or her genes – sometimes these factors can be even more important. For instance, diet affects a person's height and build, as well as the instructions in his or her genes. Likewise, family background, and income, will dictate whether or not a child who has the potential to be a brilliant musician actually gets to play an instrument and have piano or violin lessons.

Wrong again?

Predicting the future is never easy. The veteran genetic pioneer James Watson, an enthusiastic advocate of genetic enhancement, has said, 'If we can make better human beings by knowing how to add genes, why shouldn't we do it? The biggest ethical problem we have is not using that knowledge.' Watson may be right. But his vision of a genetically enhanced future could turn out to be as wrong as those scientists from the 1950s who predicted cities on the Moon and a diet of energy pills for citizens wearing silver jumpsuits and gravity boots – all by 2001!

Cloning

Another area of genetic research that may well have an impact on society is cloning – that is the creation of genetically identical living things. In 1997 Dolly the sheep was the first large mammal to be successfully cloned. Many people now think that it is only a matter of time before scientists succeed in cloning a human being. In 2002 a religious movement called the Raëlians announced that they had cloned a baby girl at a laboratory they funded. The announcement provoked worldwide media coverage. However the Raëlians failed to produce convincing evidence of this baby clone and TV and newspaper journalists doubted the claim.

Claude Vorilhon, founder of the Raëlian movement, who announced in 2002, to great scepticism, that they had cloned the world's first human. The organization's members believe that life on earth was created by visitors from another planet and that humanity's survival depends on cloning.

There are two possible uses for cloning. Firstly, individuals may seek to have themselves cloned. This procedure is possible but, at the time of writing, fraught with danger. Dolly was one success out of hundreds of failures. All her previous clone brothers and sisters were miscarried, stillborn or malformed live births. Crucially, the experiment with Dolly indicated that a clone offspring might inherit its parent's age as well as physical appearance. Dolly died young from ailments normally associated with older sheep. This suggests that any 40-year-old humans seeking to clone themselves might bring children into the world who would develop illnesses appropriate to their parents' ages rather than their own.

Secondly, in the future it could become common practice for parents to take a cell sample from each newborn child. If that child were killed, they might be able to have another child who would be very similar, through this new cloning technology. Other, more sinister possibilities could also arise. For example, a totalitarian regime could choose to clone a famous and brilliant scientist from their own or another country, and make the clone work for them – even if this required them to wait 20 years until the clone reached adulthood!

In fact clones have existed in nature since humankind began – they are called identical twins. Such twins come from the same fertilized egg, and have the same genes, in the same way a clone would. Although identical twins often look very similar, they invariably have very different characters and abilities. This is yet another reminder that nurture (the way a child is brought up and how different experiences affect his or her character) is often just as important as nature (the genes the child is born with).

Dolly, the first ever cloned sheep, suffered from arthritis at a young age. Dolly had a noticably shorter life than a 'normal' sheep.

DEBATE

Would you want to have a genetically enhanced child? If you did, could you feel proud of your child's achievements as a student, athlete or musician?

4: Food and Farming

There is another area of genetic engineering considered by some to be even more controversial than designer babies – genetically modified food, otherwise known as GM food. This is not surprising. After all, it affects everyone, whether they like it or not. We all have to eat, and it is now virtually impossible to eat a diet that is totally free of GM food.

GM food has been called 'Frankenfood' by its opponents, after Dr Frankenstein's man-made monster which turned on its creator. The comparison may sound extreme. However, while genetic modification may be a great help to farmers, it could also lead to major ecological problems.

What is it?

GM food tastes and looks just like ordinary food; the difference is at a microscopic level. Genes from other living things have been added to its genetic make-up. This is not entirely new. Farmers have been experimenting with hybrids – trying to breed animals or plants from different species – for centuries. A mule,

GM crops have been grown in the USA for many years. This is a field of weedkiller-resistant canola (also known as oilseed rape) growing in Idaho.

These genetically modified 'Flavr Savr' tomatoes last longer than non-GM tomatoes.

for example, is a cross between a horse and a donkey. Mules are sturdier and more placid than either a horse or donkey, so the mix can be beneficial. Tigers and lions can breed too, if kept in captivity together. All the offspring of mixed-species couplings are sterile (that is, they cannot have their own babies), so these new mixtures of genes can never be passed on. But genetic engineering enables food scientists to introduce genes that could never be introduced by natural means.

Why do this? Because these genetically modified plants may provide cheaper and more plentiful supplies of food, and greater profits for the food producers. At the moment, most GM crops are engineered for two purposes. One is to resist the pests that eat them. The other is to help the crops to survive undamaged when a farmer uses weedkiller to destroy other unwanted plants growing alongside them.

GM food can also be designed to last longer on the supermarket shelf, or to resist weather damage such as drought or frost. For example, flounder fish have an 'anti-freeze' gene in their blood which helps them survive in freezing water. If this gene is added to soft fruit such as strawberries, it offers them protection from frost, which would otherwise damage them. Sometimes genetically engineering food involves taking out a gene rather than adding it. Tomatoes, for example, produce a chemical that makes them go soft once they turn red. If the gene that instructs the tomato to produce this chemical is 'turned off', then the tomato stays fresher for much longer.

Animals can be genetically modified too. As we have seen, chickens have been created which have no feathers. Some pigs and salmon have also been engineered with a gene to make them grow quicker. This means they are ready to eat sooner, and more animals can be produced for food in any particular year. At the time of writing, these animal foods are still at the experimental stage, and have not been sold in the shops.

How is it done?

As you might expect, the process of creating GM food is expensive and complicated. Here is an example of what could be done. A flounder gene can be added to a strawberry to protect it from frost damage. This diagram has been simplified considerably.

1. The flounder's 'anti-freeze' gene is inserted into the DNA of a bacterium.

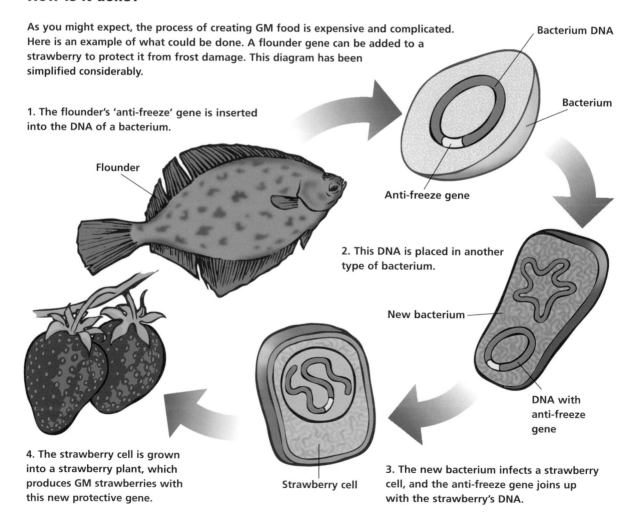

Bacterium DNA

Bacterium

Anti-freeze gene

Flounder

2. This DNA is placed in another type of bacterium.

New bacterium

DNA with anti-freeze gene

4. The strawberry cell is grown into a strawberry plant, which produces GM strawberries with this new protective gene.

Strawberry cell

3. The new bacterium infects a strawberry cell, and the anti-freeze gene joins up with the strawberry's DNA.

CASE STUDY

Sometimes genetic engineering has effects that scientists have not predicted. For instance, in 1992 a company producing GM foods added genes from Brazil nuts to their beans, to make the beans more nutritious. They were, but some people are allergic to nuts and come out in a rash, or even have a life-threatening reaction, when they eat them. These people were also allergic to the beans with nut genes, so the product was dropped.

In the shops

The first GM food experiments began in 1973, and GM foods have been sold in shops for years. Almost everyone has eaten them. Many processed foods, such as biscuits and cakes, contain GM soy and rapeseed oil. GM soya beans and rapeseed oil are also used in margarines and cooking oils.

The United States was very quick to adopt GM crops. The first products were tested in field trials in the early 1990s, and by 1995 half the corn and soya beans produced in the USA had been planted with GM seeds. Between 1994 and 2003, American farmers grew more than 3.5 trillion GM plants.

Great advances

GM food might turn out to be one of the most important developments in farming since the Agricultural Revolution of the eighteenth century, when new equipment and techniques led to a great increase in the amount of food a farmer could produce. Crop farmers, for example, are constantly battling the insect pests that damage or destroy their crops before they are ready to harvest. Genetic engineering can create crops that kill these pests before they can damage the crops. For example, maize plants have been designed to produce a poison that kills their greatest enemy, the corn borer. This poison, found naturally in bacteria in the soil, does not affect humans. This is good news for farmers, because it enables them to grow more crops. It could be especially good news for millions of people in the poorer parts of the world, who do not have enough to eat.

In Africa and parts of Asia, crops are often destroyed or damaged by poor soil, lack of rain, or a plague of pests. GM crops can be designed to combat all these problems. The current

government of India, for instance, sees GM food as the answer to their country's occasional problem of not having enough food to feed its population. Famine still causes dreadful suffering in some regions of the world. Maybe GM food is part of the solution.

Despite this hope, many commentators doubt that such benefits will be realized. This is because farming methods in poorer parts of the world are quite different from those in, for example, the USA and Europe. In Africa and parts of Asia, there are many small-scale farmers who may not be able to afford these crops. Also, there is great suspicion that small farmers who use GM crops will then become dependent on foreign GM crop producers, who will charge an unfairly high price for their seeds.

The arguments for and against GM food are very complicated. One of the advantages of crops engineered to withstand pests is that they require little or no pesticide. However, while opponents argue that genetic modification harms other creatures, supporters point out that pesticides probably do much more damage to the surrounding environment. Crop trials carried out in the UK over 2003 and onwards seem to suggest

Malnourished Malawian children are fed a maize and soya porridge by their mothers at a health centre. Supporters of genetic engineering in farming believe it will help to reduce hunger in the developing world.

that some GM crops are more harmful to wildlife than others. And there are general indications that using GM crops will reduce both the numbers and variety of countryside creatures such as butterflies, bees and birds. The long-term environmental effects of this reduction are difficult to estimate, but most biologists agree that this would have a negative effect on the environment.

Not so simple

Although the companies that create GM foods test them thoroughly, there may be dangers that are difficult to predict. For instance, it is quite possible for pollen from GM crops to be blown by the wind to nearby non-GM crops. Insects such as bees can also carry pollen from GM crops to non-GM crops up to 26 kilometres away. For these reasons, it is almost impossible to keep GM food crops from fertilizing non-GM food crops in nearby fields. The results of a mixing of natural and GM crops might be harmless, but could produce a plant that was deeply damaging to its environment. For example, a gene inserted into a plant to help it resist a powerful herbicide might transfer to a weed, creating a 'super-weed' that would be very difficult to kill. For all these reasons, some environmental organizations are so concerned about GM plants fertilizing other plants that activists try to destroy open-air crops when they are planted in scientific trials.

In addition, opponents of GM food argue that creating crops and animals that would never naturally exist in nature might lead to other problems. For example, the poison added to maize to kill the corn borer also kills monarch butterflies, which do not harm the maize at all. This has happened in experiments, although it might not happen in the wild. There are also fears that this maize is releasing unhealthy amounts of poison into the soil, and damaging it.

PERSPECTIVES

'No one will fund environmental genetic modification ... these days. I was told: the Greens have frightened off the public funds, and the private funders have gone back to inventing new chemical sprays because they get less flak that way.'

Pro-GM food author, Matt Ridley, April 2003

Modifying food to make it more nutritious might also produce other chemicals in that food which could harm people. For instance, a gene added to a potato to make it grow bigger could also make it poisonous. Like some carcinogens (substances that cause cancer), these chemicals might take many years to have a bad effect, but by then it would be too late to warn the millions of people who have been eating them.

Complex issues

Nature is a complex, interconnected web, and tampering with one aspect may lead to unexpected consequences in other areas. For example, destroying a pest that eats crops may lead to an infestation by another pest, because the first pest also ate the second pest.

It is difficult to predict how GM food will affect the world over the next few decades. North America embraced GM food farming, but now some American consumers are beginning to express concern. European farmers have never been great supporters, not least because many European shoppers have always been very suspicious of GM foods. Central and South America, Africa and Asia may be the areas of greatest expansion. China, especially, has shown great interest in using GM crops, especially disease- and pest-resistant rice and wheat which are now widely cultivated there.

A monarch butterfly rests on an aster. Butterflies and bees play a vital role in pollinating plants, and many experts argue that their numbers would be reduced if GM crops were widely planted in Europe. There are also concerns about insects carrying pollen across large distances, leading to harmful cross-pollination between GM and non-GM crops.

PERSPECTIVES

'One of the things we are forever being promised by the [biotechnology] industry is that GM crops reduce the need for chemicals in agriculture. In theory, that is hard to believe, given that most GM crops have been engineered for resistance to chemicals so they can withstand liberal applications. In practice, the situation in North America has been much worse, with unintended breeding between different GM varieties leading to super-weeds, so virulent that powerful chemicals are needed to tackle them.'

Zac Goldsmith, editor of the Ecologist *magazine, October 2003*

Anti-GM food protesters destroying oilseed rape plants in 2002.

DEBATE

So far there is no evidence to suggest that GM crops harm the people who eat them. Are protesters right to be concerned about their use?

5: Brave New World?

The science of genetic engineering is growing every day. An Internet site containing the 3 billion letter code for the human genome has around 600,000 visits a week from scientists in over 120 countries. Genetic engineering is even creating new branches of science. One is functional genomics, which aims to find out how genes do what they do. Another is bioinformatics, the study of massive computer databases needed to handle the billions of tiny but significant pieces of information contained in the genome of any living thing. Genetic engineering may – or may not – turn out to be one of the most significant discoveries in human history.

More to learn

What we currently know only represents a small fraction of what there is to learn about the extraordinary micro-complexities of genetics. Although we can now identify genes for specific personal traits or illnesses, this is only the beginning of understanding how a particular gene works.

This sequence of lines and spaces shows the DNA code of a multiple sclerosis patient.

Inside a cell there are other fragments of genetic material separate from chromosomes, such as RNA (ribonucleic acid). It has recently been discovered that RNA plays a significant role in determining how genes function. DNA depends on RNA to tell it what to do. We also know very little about how genes work together with other genes. For instance, adding a supposedly beneficial gene to a 'designer baby' may have the effect of 'turning off' another useful gene, or interacting with other genes in a way that produces an unexpectedly negative result.

Big profits?

There are billions of dollars to be made from genetic engineering. Over the next few decades the search for profits will largely dictate the areas in which most research is carried out. For example, if engineering 'designer babies' becomes an acceptable and safe medical procedure, then vast sums will be spent on further research into this aspect. Other areas, such as research into genetic illnesses, may suffer.

CASE STUDY

Every year new research brings scientists closer to understanding how DNA works, and how it can be manipulated by genetic engineering. In December 2002 a group of organizations, including the Wellcome Trust and the Washington University School of Medicine, announced that research into the genome of a mouse had revealed a 99 per cent match with the human genome. In other words, nearly all our genes are directly similar to those of a mouse. This research provides further proof that it is not the genes themselves that make one living thing a mouse, and another a human, but the way these genes work together and are controlled by other chemicals within our DNA.

At the moment, research companies are trying to patent various genes, and types of gene technology, in the same way as they have patented medicines. Such companies, and other science-based businesses which are investing in genetic research, argue that they need to protect the fruits of their research. After all, with such high research costs, the rewards need to be high too – so as to justify the risk.

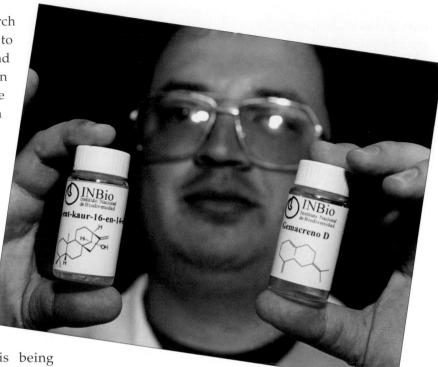

A biologist holding vials of plant extracts collected in the forests of Costa Rica. These will be studied for possible use in the manufacture of highly profitable pharmaceuticals, perfumes or natural insecticides.

Some of this research is being carried out on genetic material gathered from plants, animals and people in remote parts of Africa and South America. Biotechnology companies hope to find useful genetic traits that they can develop into profitable medicines. This is known as bioprospecting. While such activity may produce a cure for cancer or AIDS, critics see it as another way in which western nations exploit poorer countries.

To eat or not to eat?

At the time of writing, the issue of genetically modified food remains highly controversial. In Europe, some supermarkets openly boast that their food contains no GM food products. Supporters of GM food argue that this opposition is based on irrational suspicion rather than any sound evidence. Perhaps they have a point? A genetically engineered strain of rice, containing a high level of vitamin A, was created in 1990. The inventor, Ingo Potrykus, gave up his rights to the rice, and persuaded biotechnology companies that produced the rice to give it away free to poor countries. Here, it was hoped, the extra vitamin A content would save the eyesight of hundreds of thousands of children, who go blind due to a poor diet lacking this essential vitamin. Over a decade later, the rice is still under investigation and has not yet been approved by international food regulatory organizations. Meanwhile, pesticides and herbicides (which have been proven to damage the environment) are used, when it has been shown that many GM crops require less of this harmful chemical protection.

Cloning

Around one in ten couples is infertile – that is, they cannot have children. There is a huge demand for fertility treatment among this unlucky number. And, as the process of cloning becomes more widely understood, perhaps this will become another growth area for genetic science. The genes of beauty queens and college professors have already been offered for sale to infertile men and women, but it seems that most couples who would consider cloning would want their baby to be like them – so cloning one or the other partner seems to be the way forward

Two of the first goats to be cloned. In the future, animal cloning is set to become commonplace.

here. This is only likely to happen if the issue of a clone's age and cell age can be solved (see page 29, on the premature death of Dolly the sheep). After all, few parents would want to bring a child into the world whose cells were 30 or 40 years older than their actual age.

For the moment it seems that the most likely use for cloning technology will be with animals – in farming or other areas. A cloned racehorse called Promotea was born in 2003. She was the only live birth in 841 embryos created using the skin cells of two thoroughbred racehorses and eggs from a local slaughterhouse. Like Dolly the sheep, the horse is expected to age unnaturally fast, but could still offer a racehorse owner several years of top-class racing.

Cloned chicken embryos are already on sale over the Internet. Engineered to hatch, grow and mature at exactly the same rate, such products are designed to make farming more efficient. The issue of growing old prematurely is not a problem for animals produced to be eaten, as long as they taste as good as their naturally born peers.

Mass destruction

One of the most sinister potential uses for genetic engineering would be in the creation of new bioweapons. Deadly viruses, for example, could perhaps be tailor-made to attack specific racial groups. This may seem like a bizarre racist fantasy, but research was carried out in South Africa, before the collapse of the apartheid system, on a virus that would attack only black people. With the world increasingly divided along cultural and religious lines, such a weapon might be further developed either

CASE STUDY

The UK Biobank is a project funded by the British government and drug companies. It intends to collect the DNA of half a million volunteers and then follow their life histories. With such a large sample, it is hoped that clearer links will emerge between a person's genes and his or her medical history. Projects such as this will give researchers in the field of genetic engineering massively important data to work on. The more scientists know about genes, the more they can learn how to manipulate them.

One well-known bioweapon is the bacterial disease anthrax, which can be produced in powder form and sent by post to any target. In 2001, letters containing anthrax were sent to US government officials and media outlets, killing five people. Here, security personnel arrive at the US Embassy in Copenhagen, Denmark, after American diplomats received a letter containing suspicious powder, exactly a year after the 11 September 2001 attack on the World Trade Center in New York.

by terrorists or by unscrupulous governments. In 2002 it was announced that a laboratory had recreated the now virtually extinct polio virus from a blueprint obtained from the Internet and from strands of DNA bought via mail order. The announcement caused an uproar, and it was immediately suggested that the genetic codes for the more dangerous viruses be removed from public access.

The cutting edge of medicine

What is certain is that genetics will continue to be at the cutting edge of medical research. Since work began on sequencing the human genome there have been more than 350 medical advances that have made direct use of this information. Most of these – diagnostic tests, vaccines, new drugs and treatments – are still at the testing stage, but the potential for progress is huge.

Stem cell research (see pages 15-17) seems the most exciting area of development. Damaged hearts that repair themselves, severed nerves in a brain-damaged patient that can recover, spinal injuries such as those suffered by the American actor Christopher Reeve that can heal up, new limbs for amputation victims – the possibilities seem limitless. It is difficult to say how this new technology will develop. The potential of stem cell therapies is still unclear, and there is great controversy among scientists as to their worth. In the United States the political climate does not favour this research. Many 'pro-life' conservatives condemn any experimentation that involves the destruction of human embryos. But in other countries, such as China and the UK, funding and regulations regarding stem cell research are less restrictive.

However other areas of medical research have brought disappointment. The genes for such crippling diseases as muscular dystrophy and cystic fibrosis have been located, but researchers are still nowhere near finding a cure. In other illnesses known to have a strong genetic link, such as schizophrenia, specific genes contributing to this condition have yet to be found.

Foggy future?

The completion of the human genome in April 2003 opened a new chapter in this science. Many hopes and fears about DNA research have already proved to be unfounded. The actual rewards are still years away. For example, there is usually a 10-year gap between initial successful laboratory tests and drugs becoming available for patients. This gap will also apply to any genetic breakthroughs predicted in the next few years. Knowing which genes cause a disease is no guarantee of finding a cure for that disease. But knowing what the enemy is, and where to locate it, gives medical researchers fresh hope for the future.

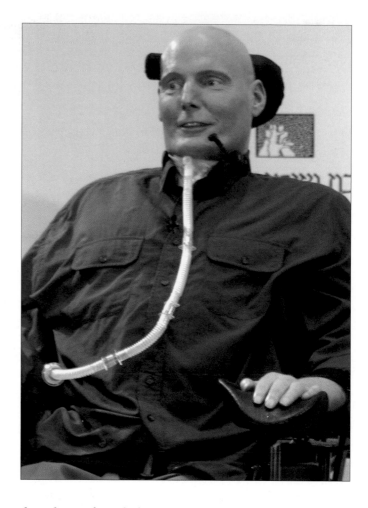

Christopher Reeve, who became famous as the actor who played Superman, was paralysed after a riding accident in January 2000. For people in his situation, stem cell research offers another chance. Perhaps these cells will one day be used to 'regrow' the damaged sections of their spinal cords?

PERSPECTIVES

'I would rather see a great social and political debate [...] than simply putting information out there and letting individuals decide.'

British geneticist and Nobel Prize winner, Sir Paul Nurse, 2003

PERSPECTIVES

'We shouldn't expect immediate major breakthroughs, but there is no doubt we have embarked on one of the most exciting chapters in the book of life.'

Sanger Institute director, Allan Bradley, 2003

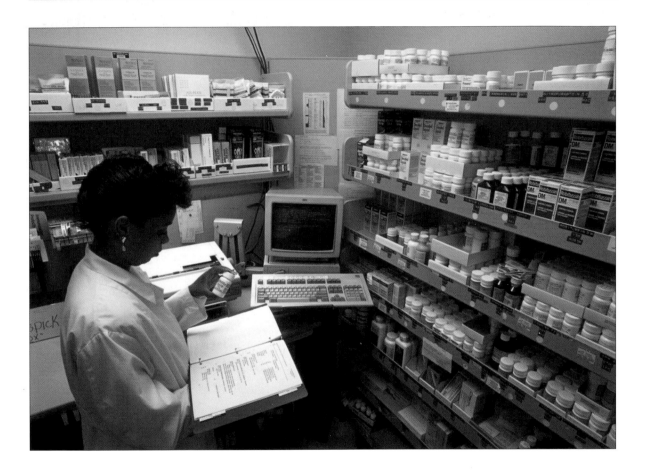

A pharmacist selects prescription drugs for a patient. Today's genetic engineering could provide tomorrow's cures for disease but years of research and tests will be needed before new drugs appear on pharmacists' shelves.

DEBATE

Should companies that have spent millions of dollars on genetic research be allowed to patent the genes they discover?

Glossary

Alzheimer's disease a condition that affects the brain in many older people, and causes severe mental and physical deterioration.

amniotic fluid the fluid surrounding the foetus, in its mother's womb.

bacteria single-celled living things, many of which cause disease.

biology a branch of science which studies living things.

bioprospecting gathering genetic material from plants, animals and people in remote parts of Africa and South America, in the hope of finding useful genetic traits that can be developed into profitable medicines.

bioweapons viruses that have been genetically engineered for use as weapons, e.g. to target a particular ethnic group.

cell the basic building block of any living thing. Every cell contains a control centre called a nucleus, which tells the cell what to do, and also contains DNA.

characteristics particular attributes which make one living thing different from another.

chromosome a tiny rod-shaped structure inside a cell, which carries DNA.

clone a genetically identical copy of another living thing.

cystic fibrosis an inherited disease that causes the lungs to become clogged with mucus.

DNA a chemical that makes up genes.

egg a female reproductive cell that can join with a male sperm cell and make a new living thing.

embryo an egg that has been fertilized and is growing into a baby.

evolution how successive generations of animals and plants can gradually change, over millions of years, to adapt to their environment.

fallopian tube a tiny tube which carries an egg from the ovary (where it was formed) to the womb, where it will grow if it is fertilized.

gene a section of DNA which gives a particular characteristic to a living thing.

genome a complete set of genes for a particular living thing.

herbicide a chemical used in agriculture designed to destroy unwanted plants.

inheritance the passing on of particular traits and characteristics through genes, from one plant or animal generation to another.

inherited diseases diseases that are passed on from parent to child.

malformed (of a baby) being faulty or abnormal.

multiple sclerosis a disease of the nervous system that causes paralysis and problems with speech, vision and co-ordination.

muscular dystrophy an inherited disease that causes increasing wasting and weakening of the muscles.

nucleus the control centre of a cell.

Parkinson's disease a disease of the nervous system that causes tremors and lack of co-ordination of the limbs.

patent to get a legal document recognizing an invention, and giving the inventor the sole right to make use of, or sell, that invention.

pesticide a chemical used in agriculture, designed to destroy insects harmful to plants.

pharming using genetically engineered animals or plants to make medicine.

schizophrenia a mental disease marked by a breakdown in the connection between thoughts, feelings and actions, and frequently accompanied by false beliefs.

sperm a male cell that fertilizes an egg to produce a new living thing.

stillborn born dead.

technology the practical use of scientific knowledge, usually in industry or commerce.

Useful Addresses

www.green-alliance.org.uk/
Green Alliance

www.greenpeace.org
Greenpeace International

www.ornl.gov/hgmis
Human Genome Project

www.monsanto.com
Monsanto

www.ncbe.reading.ac.uk
National Centre for Biotechnology Education, AMS

www.nmsi.ac.uk
National Museum of Science and Industry
www.novartis.com
Novartis

www.FoodSafety.gov
United States Food and Drugs Administration

Further Reading

The Usborne Internet-Linked Introduction to Genes and DNA
Anna Claybourne
(Usborne, 2003)

Genetics (21st Century Debates series)
Paul Dowswell
(Hodder Wayland, 2000)

Genetic Engineering (Moral Dilemmas series)
Sally Morgan
(Evans, 1998)

For older readers

Enough: Genetic Engineering and the end of Human Nature
Bill McKibben
(Bloomsbury, 2003)

Nature Via Nurture: Genes, Experience and What Makes Us Human
Matt Ridley
(Fourth Estate, 2003)

In The Blood – God, Genes and Destiny
Steve Jones
(Flamingo, 1996)

The Language of Genes
Steve Jones
(Flamingo, 1994)

Redesigning Humans
Gregory Stock
(Houghton Mifflin, 2003)

DNA: The Secret of Life
James D. Watson and Andrew Berry
(Heinemann, 2003)

Sexing The Parrot – Changing the World with DNA
Dr Wilson Wall
(Cassell, 1999)

Index

Numbers in **bold** refer to pictures.